The School for Wives

Moliere

The School for Wives

Table of Contents

The School for Wives

Moliere

Kessinger Publishing reprints thousands of hard–to–find books!

Visit us at http://www.kessinger.net

(L'Ecole des Femmes)

DRAMATIS PERSONÆ

Arnolphe, *alias* M. de La Souche.
Chrysalde, *friend to Arnolphe*.
Horace, *in love with Agnès*.
Enrique, *brother–in–law of Chrysalde*.
Oronte, *father to Horace and a great friend of Arnolphe*.
Alain, *a country fellow, servant to Arnolphe*.
A Notary.
Agnès, *a young innocent girl, brought up by Arnolphe*.
Georgette, *a country–woman, servant to Arnolphe*.

Scene.—A Square in a Town

The School for Wives

ACT I

Scene I.—Chrysalde, Arnolphe.

Chrysalde. You have come to marry her, you say?

Arnolphe. Yes, I mean to settle the business tomorrow.

Chrysalde. We are here alone, and I think we can speak together without fear of being overheard. Do you wish me to open my heart to you like a friend? Your plan makes me tremble with fear for you. To take a wife is a rash step for you, whichever way you consider the matter.

Arnolphe. True, my friend. Possibly you find in your own home reasons why you should fear for me. I fancy that your own forehead shows that horns are everywhere the infallible accompaniment of marriage.

Chrysalde. These are accidents against which we cannot insure ourselves; it seems to me that the trouble people take about this is very ridiculous. But when I fear for you, it is on account of this raillery of which a hundred poor husbands have felt the sting. For you know that neither great nor small have been safe from your criticism; that your greatest pleasure, wherever you are, is to make a mighty outcry about secret intrigues—

Arnolphe. Exactly. Is there another city in the world where husbands are so patient as here? Do we not meet with them in every variety, and well provided with everything? One heaps up wealth, which his wife shares with those who are eager to make him a dupe; another, slightly more fortunate, but not less infamous, sees his wife receive presents day after day, and is not troubled in mind by any jealous twinge when she tells him that they are the rewards of virtue. One makes a great noise, which does him not the slightest good; another lets matters take their course in all meekness, and, seeing the gallant arrive at his house, very politely takes up his gloves and his cloak. One married woman cunningly pretends to make a confident of her confiding husband, who slumbers securely under such a delusion, and pities the gallant for his pains, which, however, the latter does not throw away. Another married woman, to account for her extravagance, says that the money she spends has been won at play; and the silly husband, without considering at what play, thanks Heaven for her winnings. In short, we find subjects for satire everywhere, and may I, as a spectator, not laugh at them? Are not these fools—

Chrysalde. Yes; but he who laughs at another must beware, lest he in turn be laughed at himself. I hear what is said, and how some folks delight in retailing what goes on; but no one has seen me exult at reports, which are bruited about in the places I frequent. I am rather reserved in this respect; and, though I might condemn a certain toleration of these matters, and am resolved by no means to suffer quietly what some husbands endure, yet I have never affected to say so; for, after all, satire may fall upon ourselves, and we should never vow in such cases what we should or should not do. Thus, if by an overruling fate, some natural disgrace should ever happen to my brow, I am almost sure, after the way in which I have acted, that people would be content to laugh at it in their sleeve; and possibly, in addition, I may reap this advantage, that a few good fellows will say "What a pity!" But with you, my dear friend, it is otherwise. I tell you again you are running a plaguy risk. As your tongue has always persistently bantered husbands accused of being tolerant; as you have shown yourself like a demon let loose upon them, you must walk straight for fear of being made a laughing–stock; and, if it happens that they get the least pretext, take care they do not publish your disgrace at the public market–cross, and —

Arnolphe. Good Heaven, friend, do not trouble yourself. He will be a clever man who catches me in this way. I know all the cunning tricks and subtle devices which women use to deceive us, and how one is fooled by their dexterity, and I have taken precautions against this mischance. She whom I am marrying possesses all the innocence which may protect my forehead from evil influence.

Chrysalde. Why, what do you imagine? That a silly girl, to be brief —

Arnolphe. To marry a silly girl is not to become silly myself. I believe, as a good Christian, that your better half is very wise; but a clever wife is ominous, and I know what some people have to pay for choosing theirs with too much talent. What, I go and saddle myself with an intellectual woman, who talks of nothing but of her assembly and *ruelle*; who writes tender things in prose and in verse, and is visited by Marquises and wits, whilst, as "Mrs. So–and–so's husband, " I should be like a saint, whom no one calls upon! No, no, I will have none of your lofty minds. A woman who writes knows more than she ought to do. I intend that my wife shall not even be clever enough to know what a rhyme is. If one plays at *corbillon* with her, and asks her in her turn "What is put into

3

the basket, " I will have her answer, "A cream tart. " In a word, let her be very ignorant; and to tell you the plain truth, it is enough for her that she can say her prayers, love me, saw and spin.

Chrysalde. A stupid wife, then, is your fancy?

Arnolphe. So much so that I should prefer a very stupid and ugly woman to a very beautiful one with a great deal of wit.

Chrysalde. Wit and beauty —

Arnolphe. Virtue is quite enough.

Chrysalde. But how can you expect, after, all, that a mere simpleton can ever know what it is to be virtuous? Besides, to my mind, it must be very wearisome for a man to have a stupid creature perpetually with him. Do you think you act rightly, and that, by reliance on your plan, a man's brow is saved from danger? A woman of sense may fail in her duty; but she must at least do so knowingly; a stupid woman may at any time fail in hers, without desiring or thinking of it.

Arnolphe. To this fine argument, this deep discourse, I reply as Pantagruel did to Panurge: Urge me to marry any other woman than a stupid one; preach and lecture till Whitsuntide, you shall be amazed to find, when you have done, that you have not persuaded me in the very slightest.

Chrysalde. I do not want to say another word.

Arnolphe. Every man has his own way. With my wife, as in everything, I mean to follow my fashion. I think I am rich enough to take a partner who shall owe all to me, and whose humble station and complete dependence cannot reproach me either with her poverty or her birth. A sweet and staid look made me love Agnès, amongst other children, when she was only four. It came into my mind to ask her from her mother, who was very poor; the good country–woman, learning my wish, was delighted to rid herself of the charge. I had her brought up, according to my own notions, in a little solitary convent; that is to say, directing them what means to adopt in order to make her as idiotic as possible. Thank Heaven, success has crowned my efforts; and I am very thankful to say, I have found her

4

so innocent that I have blessed Heaven for having done what I wished, in giving me a wife according to my desire. Then I brought her away; and as my house is continually open to a hundred different people, and as we must be on our guard against everything, I have kept her in another house where no one comes to see me; and where her good disposition cannot be spoiled, as she meets none but people as simple as herself. You will say, "Wherefore this long story? " It is to let you see the care I have taken. To crown all, and as you are a trusty friend, I ask you to sup with her to-night. I wish you would examine her a little, and see if I am to be condemned for my choice.

Chrysalde. With all my heart.

Arnolphe. You can judge of her looks and her innocence when you converse with her.

Chrysalde. As to that, what you have told me cannot —

Arnolphe. What I have told you falls even short of the truth:

I admire her simplicity on all occasions; sometimes she says things at which I split my sides with laughing. The other day—would you believe it?—she was uneasy, and came to ask me, with unexampled innocence, if children came through the ears.

Chrysalde. I greatly rejoice, M. Arnolphe —

Arnolphe. What! will you always call me by that name?

Chrysalde. Ah, it comes to my lips in spite of me; I never remember M. de la Souche. Who on earth has put it into your head to change your name at forty-two years of age, and give yourself a title from a rotten old tree on your farm?

Arnolphe. Besides the fact that the house is known by that name, la Souche pleases my ear better than Arnolphe.

Chrysalde. What a pity to give up the genuine name of one's fathers, and take one based on chimeras! Most people have an itching that way, and, without including you in the comparison, I knew a country-fellow called Gros-Pierre, who, having no other property but a rood of land, had a muddy ditch made all around it, and took the high-sounding name of M. de l'Isle.

Arnolphe. You might dispense with such examples. But, at all events, de la Souche is the name I bear. I have a reason for it, I like it; and to call me otherwise is to annoy me.

Chrysalde. Most people find it hard to fall in with it; I even yet see letters addressed —

Arnolphe. I endure it easily from those who are not informed; but you —

Chrysalde. Be it so; we will make no difficulty about that; I will take care to accustom my lips to call you nothing else than M. de la Souche.

Arnolphe. Farewell. I am going to knock here, to wish them good morning, and simply to say that I have come back.

Chrysalde (aside). Upon my word, I think he is a perfect fool.

Arnolphe (alone). He is a little touched on certain points. Strange, to see how each man is passionately fond of his own opinion. (*Knocks at his door.*) Hulloa!

Scene II.—Arnolphe, Alain, Georgette, *within* .

Alain.—Who knocks?

Arnolphe. Open the door! (*Aside.*) I think they will be very glad to see me after ten days' absence.

Alain. Who is there?

Arnolphe. I.

Alain. Georgette!

Georgette. Well!

Alain. Open the door there!

Georgette. Go, and do it yourself!

Alain. You go and do it!

Georgette. Indeed, I shall not go.

Alain. No more shall I.

Arnolphe. Fine compliments, while I am left without. Hulloa! Here, please.

Georgette. Who knocks?

Arnolphe. Your master.

Georgette. Alain!

Alain. What!

Georgette. It is the master. Open the door quickly.

Alain. Open it yourself.

Georgette. I am blowing the fire.

Alain. I am taking care that the sparrow does not go out, for fear of the cat.

Arnolphe. Whoever of you two does not open the door shall have no food for four days. Ah!

Georgette. Why do you come when I was running?

Alain. Why should you more than I? A pretty trick indeed!

Georgette. Stand out of the way.

Alain. Stand out of the way yourself.

Georgette. I wish to open the door.

Alain. And so do I.

Georgette. You shall not.

Alain. No more shall you.

Georgette. Nor you.

Arnolphe. I need have patience here.

Alain (*entering*). There; it is I, master.

Georgette (*entering*). Your servant; it is I.

Alain. If it were not out of respect for master here, I —

Arnolphe (*receiving a push from* Alain). Hang it!

Alain. Pardon me.

Arnolphe. Look at the lout!

Alain. It was she also, master —

Arnolphe. Hold your tongues, both of you. Just answer me and let us have no more fooling. Well, Alain, how is every one here?

Alain. Master, we — (Arnolphe *takes off* Alain'S *hat*). Master, we — (Arnolphe *takes it off again.*) Thank Heaven, we —

Arnolphe (*taking off the hat a third time and flinging it on the ground*). Who taught you, impertinent fool, to speak to me with your hat on your head?

Alain. You are right; I am wrong.

Arnolphe (*to* Alain). Ask Agnès to come down.

Scene III.—Arnolphe, Georgette.

Arnolphe. Was she sad after I went away?

Georgette. Sad? No.

Arnolphe. No?

Georgette. Yes, yes.

Arnolphe. Why, then?

Georgette. May I die on the spot, but she expected to see you return every minute; and we never heard a horse, an ass, or a mule pass by without her thinking it was you.

Scene IV.—Arnolphe, Agnès, Alain, Georgette.

Arnolphe. Work in hand? That is a good sign. Well, Agnès, I have returned. Are you glad of it?

Agnès. Yes, sir, Heaven be thanked.

Arnolphe. I too am glad to see you again. You have always been well? I see you have.

Agnès. Except for the fleas, which troubled me in the night.

Arnolphe. Ah, you shall soon have some one to drive them away.

Agnès. I shall be pleased with that.

Arnolphe. I can easily imagine it. What are you doing there?

Agnès. I am making myself some caps. Your nightshirts and caps are finished.

Arnolphe. Ah, that is all right. Well, go up stairs. Do not tire yourself. I will soon return, and talk to you of important matters.

Scene V.—Arnolphe, *alone.*

Heroines of the day, learned ladies, who spout tender and fine sentiments, I defy in a breath all your verses, your novels, your letters, your love–letters, your entire science, to be worth as much as this virtuous and modest ignorance. We must not be dazzled by riches; and so long as honour is—

Scene VI.—Horace, Arnolphe.

Arnolphe. What do I see? Is it—Yes. I am mistaken. But no. No; it is himself. Hor—

Horace. Mr. Arn—

Arnolphe. Horace.

Horace. Arnolphe.

Arnolphe. Ah! what joy indeed! And how long have you been here?

Horace. Nine days.

Arnolphe. Really.

Horace. I went straight to your house, but in vain.

Arnolphe. I was in the country.

Horace. Yes, you had been gone ten days.

Arnolphe. Oh, how these children spring up in a few years! I am amazed to see him so tall, after having known him no higher than that.

Horace. You see how it is.

Arnolphe. But tell me how is Oronte, your father, my good and dear friend, whom I esteem and revere? What is he doing? What is he saying? Is he still hearty? He knows I am interested in all that affects him; we have not seen one another these four years, nor, what is more, written to each other, I think.

Horace. M. Arnolphe, he is even more cheerful than we; I had a letter from him for you. But he has since informed me in another letter, that he is coming here, though as yet I do not know the reason for it. Can you tell me which of your townsmen has returned with abundance of wealth earned during a fourteen years' residence in America?

Arnolphe. No. Have you not heard his name?

Horace. Enrique.

Arnolphe. No.

Horace. My father speaks of him and his return, as though he should be well known to me; he writes that they are about to set out together, on an affair of consequence, of which his letter says nothing. (*Gives* Oronte's *letter to* Arnolphe.)

Arnolphe. I shall assuredly be very glad to see him, and shall do my best to entertain him. (*After reading the letter.*) Friends do not need to send such polite letters, and all these compliments are unnecessary. Even if he had not taken the trouble to write one word, you might have freely disposed of all I have.

Horace. I am a man who takes people at their word; and I have present need of a hundred pistoles.

Arnolphe. Upon my word, you oblige me by using me thus. I rejoice that I have them with me. Keep the purse too.

Horace. I must—

Arnolphe. Drop this ceremony. Well, how do you like this town so far?

Horace. Its inhabitants are numerous, its buildings splendid, and I should think that its amusements are wonderful.

Arnolphe. Everyone has his own pleasures, after his own fashion; but for those whom we christen our gallants, they have in this town just what pleases them, for the women are born flirts. Dark and fair are amiably disposed, and the husbands also are the most kind in the world. It is a pleasure fit for a King; to me it is a mere comedy to see the pranks I do. Perhaps you have already smitten some one. Have you had no adventure yet? Men of your figure can do more than men who have money, and you are cut out to make a cuckold.

Horace. Not to deceive you as to the simple truth, I have had a certain love–passage in these parts, and friendship compels me to tell you of it.

Arnolphe(aside). Good. Here is another queer story to set down in my pocket–book.

Horace. But pray, let these things be secret.

Arnolphe. Oh!

Horace. You know that in these matters a secret divulged destroys our expectations. I will then frankly confess to you that my heart has been smitten in this place by a certain fair maid. My little attentions were at once so successful that I obtained a pleasant introduction to her; not to boast too much, nor to do her an injustice, affairs go very well with me.

Arnolphe (laughing). Ha! ha! And she is—

Horace (pointing to the house of Agnès). A young creature living in yonder house, of which you can see the red walls from this. Simple, of a truth, through the matchless folly of a man who hides her from all the world; but who, amidst the ignorance in which he would enslave her, discloses charms that throw one into raptures, as well as a thoroughly engaging manner, and something indescribably tender, against which no heart is proof. But perhaps you have seen this young star of love, adorned by so many charms. Agnès is her name.

Arnolphe(*aside*). Oh, I shall burst with rage!

Horace. As for the man, I think his name is De la Zousse, or Souche; I did not concern myself about the name. He is rich, by what they told me, but not one of the wisest of men; they say he is a ridiculous fellow. Do you not know him?

Arnolphe(*aside*). It is a bitter pill I have to swallow!

Horace. Why, you do not speak a word.

Arnolphe. Oh, yes—I know him.

Horace. He is a fool, is he not?

Arnolphe. Ugh!

Horace. What do you say? Ugh—that means yes? Jealous, I suppose, ridiculously so? Stupid? I see he is just as they told me. To be brief, the lovely Agnes has succeeded in enslaving me. She is a pretty jewel, to tell you honestly; it would be a sin if such a rare beauty were left in the power of this eccentric fellow. For me, all my efforts, all my dearest wishes, are to make her mine in spite of this jealous wretch; and the money which I so freely borrow of you, was only to bring this laudable enterprise to a conclusion. You know better than I, that, whatever we undertake, money is the masterkey to all great plans, and that this sweet metal, which distracts so many, promotes our triumphs, in love as in war. You seem vexed? Can it be that you disapprove of my design?

Arnolphe. No; but I was thinking—

Horace. This conversation wearies you? Farewell. I will soon pay you a visit to return thanks.

Arnolphe(*thinking himself alone*). What! must it—

Horace(*returning*). Once again, pray be discreet; do not go and spread my secret abroad.

Arnolphe(*thinking himself alone*). I feel within my soul—

Horace(returning again). And above all to my father, who would perhaps get enraged, if he knew of it.

*Arnolphe(expecting*HORACE*to return again).* Oh!—

Scene VII.—Arnolphe, *alone.*

Oh, what I have endured during this conversation! Never was trouble of mind equal to mine! With what rashness and extreme haste did he come to tell me of this affair! Though my second name keeps him at fault, did ever any blunderer run on so furiously? But, having endured so much, I ought to have refrained until I had learned that which I have reason to fear, to have drawn out his foolish chattering to the end, and ascertained their secret understanding completely. Let me try to overtake him; I fancy he is not far off. Let me worm from him the whole mystery. I tremble for the misfortune which may befall me; for we often seek more than we wish to find.

ACT II

Scene I.—Arnolphe, *alone.*

It is no doubt well, when I think of it, that I have lost my way, and failed to find him; for after all, I should not have been able entirely to conceal from his eyes the overwhelming pang of my heart. The grief that preys upon me would have broken forth, and I do not wish him to know what he is at present ignorant of. But I am not the man to put up with this, and leave a free field for this young spark to pursue his design. I am resolved to check his progress, and learn, without delay, how far they understand each other. My honour is specially involved in this. I regard her already as my wife. She cannot have made a slip without covering me with shame; and whatever she does will be placed to my account. Fatal absence! Unfortunate voyage! (*Knocks at his door.*)

Scene II.—Arnolphe, Alain, Georgette.

Alain. Ah, master, this time—

Arnolphe. Peace. Come here, both of you. That way, that way. Come along, come, I tell

14

you.

Georgette. Ah, you frighten me; all my blood runs cold.

Arnolphe. Is it thus you have obeyed me in my absence? You have both combined to betray me!

Georgette(*falling at* Arnolphe's *feet*). Oh, master, do not eat me, I implore you.

Alain(*aside*). I am sure some mad dog has bitten him.

Arnolphe (*aside*). Ugh, I cannot speak, I am so filled with rage. I am choking, and should like to throw off my clothes—(*to* Alain *and* Georgette). You cursed scoundrels, you have permitted a man to come—(*to* Alain, *who tries to escape*). You would run away, would you! You must this instant—(*to* Georgette). If you move—Now I wish you to tell me—(*to* Alain). Hi!—Yes, I wish you both—(Alain *and* Georgette *rise, and again try to escape*)—Whoever of you moves, upon my word, I shall knock him down. How came that man into my house? Now speak. Make haste, quick, directly, instantly, no thinking! Will you speak?

Both. Oh, oh!

Georgette(*falling at his kness*). My heart fails me!

Alain(*falling at his knees*). I am dying.

Arnolphe(*aside*). I perspire all over. Let me take a breath. I must fan myself, and walk about. Could I believe, when I saw Horace as a little boy, that he would grow up for this? Heaven, how I suffer! I think it would be better that I should gently draw from Agnès' own mouth an account of what touches me so. Let me try to moderate my anger. Patience, my heart; softly, softly. (*To* Alain *and* Georgette.) Rice, go in, and bid Agnès come to me—Stay, her surprise would be less. They will go and tell her how uneasy I am. I will go myself and bring her out. (*To* Alain *and* Georgette.) Wait for me here.

Scene III.—Alain, Georgette.

The School for Wives

Georgette. Heavens, how terrible he is! His looks made me afraid—horribly afraid. Never did I see a more hideous Christian.

Alain. This gentleman has vexed him; I told you so.

Georgette. But what on earth is the reason that he so strictly makes us keep our mistress in the house? Why does he wish to hide her from all the world, and cannot bear to see any one approach her?

Alain. Because that makes him jealous.

Georgette. But how has he got such a fancy in his head?

Alain. Because—because he is jealous.

Georgette. Yes; but wherefore is he so? and why this anger?

Alain. Because jealousy—understand me, Georgette, jealousy is a thing—a thing—which makes people uneasy —and which drives folk all round the house. I am going to give you an example, so that you may understand the thing better. Tell me, is it not true that, when you have your broth in your hand, and some hungry person comes up to eat it, you would be in a rage, and be ready to beat him?

Georgette. Yes, I understand that.

Alain. It is just the same. Woman is in fact the broth of man; and when a man sees other folks sometimes, trying to dip their fingers in his broth, he soon displays extreme anger at it.

Georgette. Yes; but why does not every one do the same? Why do we see some who appear to be pleased when their wives are with handsome fine gentlemen?

Alain. Because every one has not the greedy love which will give nothing away.

Georgette. If I am not blind, I see him returning.

Alain. Your eyes are good; it is he.

Georgette. See how vexed he is.

Alain. That is because he is in trouble.

Scene IV.—Arnolphe, Algeorgette.

Arnolphe(*aside*). A certain Greek told the Emperor Augustus, as an axiom as useful as it was true, that when any accident puts us in a rage, we should, first of all, repeat the alphabet; so that in the interval our anger may abate, and we may do nothing that we ought not to do. I have followed his advice in the matter of Agnès; and I have brought her here designedly, under pretence of taking a walk, so that the suspicions of my disordered mind may cunningly lead her to the topic, and, by sounding her heart, gently find out the truth.

Scene V.—Arnolphe, Agnès, Alain, Georgette.

Arnolphe. Come, Agnès. (*To* Alain *and* Georgette .) Get you in.

Scene VI.—Arnolphe, Agnès.

Arnolphe. This is a nice walk.

Agnès. Very nice.

Arnolphe. What a fine day.

Agnès. Very fine.

Arnolphe. What news?

Agnès. The kitten is dead.

Arnolphe. Pity! But what then? We are all mortal, and every one is for himself. Did it rain when I was in the country?

The School for Wives

Agnès. No.

Arnolphe. Were you not wearied?

Agnès. I am never wearied.

Arnolphe. What did you do then, these nine or ten days?

Agnès. Six shirts, I think, and six nightcaps also.

Arnolphe(*after musing*). The world, dear Agnès, is a strange place. Observe the scandal, and how everybody gossips. Some of the neighbours have told me that an unknown young man came to the house in my absence; that you permitted him to see and talk to you. But I did not believe these slandering tongues, and I offered to bet that it was false—

Agnès. Oh, Heaven, do not bet; you would assuredly lose.

Arnolphe. What! It is true that a man—

Agnès. Quite true. I declare to you that he was scarcely ever out of the house.

Arnolphe(*aside*). This confession, so candidly made, at least assures me of her simplicity. (*Aloud.*) But I think, Agnès, if my memory is clear, that I forbade you to see any one.

Agnès. Yes; but you do not know why I saw him; you would doubtless have done as much.

Arnolphe. Possibly; but tell me then how it was.

Agnès. It is very wonderful, and hard to believe. I was on the balcony, working in the open air, when I saw a handsome young man passing close to me under the trees, who, seeing me look at him, immediately bowed very respectfully. I, not to be rude, made him a curtsey. Suddenly he made another bow; I quickly made another curtsey; and when he repeated it for the third time, I answered it directly with a third curtsey. He went on, returned, went past again, and each time made me another bow. And I, who was looking earnestly at all these acts of politeness, returned him as many curtseys; so that if night had not fallen just then, I should have kept on continually in that way; not wishing to yield, and have the vexation of his thinking me less civil than himself.

Arnolphe. Very good.

Agnès. Next day, being at the door, an old woman accosted me, and said to me something like this: "My child, may good Heaven bless you, and keep you long in all your beauty. It did not make you such a lovely creature to abuse its gifts; you must know that you have wounded a heart which to–day is driven to complain."

Arnolphe(*aside*). Oh, tool of Satan! damnable wretch!

Agnès. "Have I wounded any one? " I answered, quite astonished. "Yes, " she said, "wounded; you have indeed wounded a gentleman. It is him you saw yesterday from the balcony. " "Alas! " said I, "what could have been the cause? Did I, without thinking, let anything fall on him? " "No, " replied she; "it was your eyes which gave the fatal blow; from their glances came all his injury. " "Alas! good Heaven, " said I, "I am more than ever surprised. Do my eyes contain something bad, that they can give it to other people? " "Yes, " cried she, "your eyes, my girl, have a poison to hurt withal, of which you know nothing. In a word, the poor fellow pines away; and if, " continued the charitable old woman, "your cruelty refuses him assistance, it is likely he shall be carried to his grave in a couple of days. " "Bless me! " said I, "I would be very sorry for that; but what assistance does he require of me? " "My child, " said she, "he requests only the happiness of seeing and conversing with you. Your eyes alone can prevent his ruin, and cure the disease they have caused. " "Oh! gladly, " said I; "and, since it is so, he may come to see me here as often as he likes."

Arnolphe(*aside*). O cursed witch! poisoner of souls! may hell reward your charitable tricks!

Agnès. That is how he came to see me, and got cured. Now tell me, frankly, if I was not right? And could I, after all, have the conscience to let him die for lack of aid?—I, who feel so much pity for suffering people, and cannot see a chicken die without weeping!

Arnolphe(*aside*). All this comes only from an innocent soul; I blame my imprudent absence for it, which left this kindliness of heart without a protector, exposed to the wiles of artful seducers. I fear that the rascal, in his bold passion, has carried the matter somewhat beyond a joke.

Agnès. What ails you? I think you are a little angry. Was there anything wrong in what I have told you?

Arnolphe. No. But tell me what followed, and how the young man behaved during his visits.

Agnès. Alas! if you but knew how delightful he was; how he got rid of his illness as soon as I saw him, the present he made me of a lovely casket, and the money which Alain and Georgette have had from him, you would no doubt love him, and say, as we say—

Arnolphe. Yes. But what did he do when he was alone with you?

Agnès. He swore that he loved me with an unequalled passion, and said the prettiest words possible, things that nothing ever can equal, the sweetness of which charms me whenever I hear him speak, and moves I know not what within me.

Arnolphe(aside). Oh! sad inquiry into a fatal mystery, in which the inquirer alone suffers all the pain. (*Aloud.*) Besides all these speeches, all these pretty compliments, did he not also bestow a few caresses on you?

Agnès. Oh, so many! He took my hands and my arms, and was never tired of kissing them.

Arnolphe. Agnès, did he take nothing else from you? (*Seeing her confused.*) Ugh!

Agnès. Why, he—

Arnolphe. What?

Agnès. Took—

Arnolphe. Ugh!

20

Agnès. The—

Arnolphe. Well?

Agnès. I dare not tell you; you will perhaps be angry with me.

Arnolphe. No.

Agnès. Yes, but you will.

Arnolphe. Good Heavens! no.

Agnès. Swear on your word.

Arnolphe. On my word, then.

Agnès. He took my—You will be in a passion.

Arnolphe. No.

Agnès. Yes.

Arnolphe. No, no, no, no! What the devil is this mystery? What did he take from you?

Agnès. He—

Arnolphe(*aside*). I am suffering the torments of the damned.

Agnès. He took away from me the ribbon you gave me. To tell you the truth, I could not prevent him.

Arnolphe(*drawing his breath*). Oh! let the ribbon go. But I want to know if he did nothing to you but kiss your arms.

Agnès. Why! do people do other things?

Arnolphe. Not at all. But, to cure the disorder which he said had seized him, did he not ask you for any other remedy?

Agnès. No. You may judge that I would have granted him anything to do him good, if he had asked for it.

Arnolphe(aside). By the kindness of Heaven, I am cheaply out of it! May I be blessed if I fall into such a mistake again! (*Aloud*). Pooh! That is the result of your innocence, Agnès. I shall say no more about it. What is done is done. I know that, by flattering you, the gallant only wishes to deceive you, and to laugh at you afterwards.

Agnès. Oh, no! He told me so more than a score of times.

Arnolphe. Ah! you do not know that he is not to be believed. But, now, learn that to accept caskets, and to listen to the nonsense of these handsome fops, to allow them languidly to kiss your hands and charm your heart, is a mortal sin, and one of the greatest that can be committed.

Agnès. A sin, do you say? And why, pray?

Arnolphe. Why? The reason is the absolute law that Heaven is incensed by such things.

Agnès. Incensed! But why should it be incensed? Ah, it is so sweet and agreeable! How strange is the joy one feels from all this; up to this time I was ignorant of these things.

Arnolphe. Yes, all these tender passages, these pretty speeches and sweet caresses, are a great pleasure; but they must be enjoyed in an honest manner, and their sin should be taken away by marriage.

Agnès. Is it no longer a sin when one is married?

Arnolphe. No.

Agnès. Then please marry me quickly.

Arnolphe. If you wish it, I wish it also; I have returned hither for the purpose of marrying you.

Agnès. Is that possible?

Arnolphe. Yes.

Agnès. How happy you will make me!

Arnolphe. Yes, I have no doubt that marriage will please you.

Agnès. Then we two shall—

Arnolphe. Nothing is more certain.

Agnès. How I shall caress you, if this comes to pass.

Arnolphe. Ha! And I shall do the same to you.

Agnès. I can never tell when people are jesting. Do you speak seriously?

Arnolphe. Yes, you might see that I do.

Agnès. We are to be married?

Arnolphe. Yes.

Agnès. But when?

Arnolphe. This very evening.

Agnès(laughing). This very evening?

Arnolphe. This very evening. Does that make you laugh?

Agnès. Yes.

Arnolphe. To see you happy is my desire.

Agnès. Oh, how greatly I am obliged to you, and what satisfaction I shall have with him!

Arnolphe. With whom?

Agnès. With—him there—

Arnolphe. Him there! I am not speaking of him there. You are a little quick in selecting a husband. In a word, it is some one else whom I have ready for you. And as for that gentleman, I require, by your leave (though the illness of which he accuses you should be the death of him), that henceforth you break off all intercourse with him; that, when he comes to the house, you will, by way of compliment, just shut the door in his face; throw a stone out of the window at him when he knocks, and oblige him in good earnest never to appear again. Do you hear me, Agnès? I shall observe your behaviour, concealed in a recess.

Agnès. Oh dear, he is so handsome! He is—

Arnolphe. Ha! How you are talking!

Agnès. I shall not have the heart—

Arnolphe. No more chatter. Go up stairs.

Agnès. But surely! Will you—

Arnolphe. Enough. I am master; I command; do you go and obey.

ACT III

Scene I.—Arnolphe, Agnès, Alain, Georgette.

Arnolphe. Yes, all has gone well; my joy is extreme. You have obeyed my orders to perfection, and brought the fair seducer to utter confusion. See what it is to have a wise

24

counsellor. Your innocence, Agnès, had been betrayed; look what you had been brought to, before you had been aware of it. You were treading, deprived of my warning, right—down the broad path to hell and perdition. The way of all these young fops is but too well known. They have their fine rolls, plenty of ribbons and plumes, big wigs, good teeth, a smooth address; but I tell you they have the cloven foot beneath; and they are very devils, whose corrupt appetites try to prey upon the honour of women. This time, however, thanks to the care that has been taken, you have escaped with your virtue. The style in which I saw you throw that stone at him, which has dashed the hopes of all his plans, still more determines me not to delay the marriage for which I told you to prepare. But, before all, it is well I should speak a few words with you which may be salutary. (*To* Georgette *and* Alain). Bring out a chair in the open air. As for you, if you ever—

Georgette. We shall take care to remember all your instructions, that other gentleman imposed on us, but—

Alain. If he ever gets in here, may I never drink another drop. Besides he is a fool. He gave us two gold crowns the other day, which were under weight.

Arnolphe. Well, get what I ordered for supper; and as to the contract I spoke of, let one of you fetch the notary who lives at the corner of the market—place.

Scene II.—Arnolphe, Agnes.

Arnolphe(*seated*). Agnès, put your work down, and listen to me. Raise your head a little, and turn your face round. (*Putting his finger on his forehead.*) There, look at me here while I speak, and take good note of even the smallest word. I am going to wed you, Agnès; you ought to bless your stars a hundred times a day, to think of your former low estate, and at the same time, to wonder at my goodness in raising you from a poor country girl to the honourable rank of a citizen's wife; to enjoy the bed and the embraces of a man who has shunned all such trammels, and whose heart has refused to a score of women, well fitted to please, the honour which he intends to confer on you. You must always keep in mind, I say, how insignificant you would be without this glorious alliance, in order that the picture may teach you the better to merit the condition in which I shall place you, and make you always know yourself, so that I may never repent of what I am doing. Marriage, Agnès, is no joke. The position of a wife calls for strict duties; I do not mean to exalt you to that condition, in order that you may be free and take your ease.

25

The School for Wives

Your sex is formed for dependence. Omnipotence goes with the beard. Though there are two halves in the connection, yet these two halves are by no means equal. The one half is supreme, and the other subordinate: the one is all submission to the other which rules; the obedience which the well disciplined soldier shows to his leader, the servant to his master, a child to his parent, the lowest monk to his superior, is far below the docility, obedience, humility, and profound respect due from the wife to her husband, her chief, her lord, and her master. When he looks at her gravely, her duty is at once to lower her eyes, never daring to look him in the face, until he chooses to favour her with a tender glance. Our women now–a–days do not understand this; but do not be spoiled by the example of others. Take care not to imitate those miserable flirts whose pranks are talked of all over the city; and do not let the evil one tempt you, that is, do not listen to any young coxcomb. Remember, Agnès, that, in making you part of myself, I give my honour into your hands, which honour is fragile, and easily damaged; that it will not do to trifle in such a matter, and that there are boiling cauldrons in hell, into which wives who live wickedly are thrown for evermore. I am not telling you a parcel of stories; you ought to let these lessons sink into your heart. If you practice them sincerely, and take care not to flirt, your soul will ever be white and spotless as a lily; but if you stain your honour, it will become as black as coal. You will seem hideous to all, and one day you will become the devil's own property, and boil in hell to all eternity—from which may the goodness of Heaven defend you! Make a curtsey. As a novice in a convent ought to know her duties by heart, so it ought to be on getting married: here in my pocket I have an important document which will teach you the duty of a wife. I do not know the author, but it is some good soul or other; and I desire that this shall be your only study. (*Rises.*) Stay. Let me see if you can read it fairly.

Agnès(reads). *"The Maxims of Marriage; or the Duties of a Wife; together with her Daily Exercise.*

"First Maxim.

"She who is honourably wed should remember, notwithstanding the fashion now–a–days, that the man who marries does not take a wife for anyone but himself."

Arnolphe. I shall explain what that means, but at present let us only read.

Agnès(continues)—

The School for Wives

"*Second Maxim.*

"She ought not to bedeck herself more than her husband likes. The care of her beauty concerns him alone; and if others think her plain, that must go for nothing.

"*Third Maxim.*

"Far from her be the study of ogling, washes, paints, pomatums, and the thousand preparations for a good complexion. These are ever fatal poisons to honour; and the pains bestowed to look beautiful are seldom taken for a husband.

"*Fourth Maxim.*

"When she goes out, she should conceal the glances of her eyes beneath her hood, as honour requires; for in order to please her husband rightly, she should please none else.

"*Fifth Maxim.*

"It is fit that she receive none but those who visit her husband. The gallants that have no business but with the wife, are not agreeable to the husband.

"*Sixth Maxim.*

"She must firmly refuse presents from men, for in these days nothing is given for nothing.

"*Seventh Maxim.*

"Amongst her furniture, however she dislikes it, there must be neither writing–desk, ink, paper, nor pens. According to all good rules everything written in the house should be written by the husband.

"*Eighth Maxim.*

"Those disorderly meetings, called social gatherings, ever corrupt the minds of women. It is good policy to forbid them; for there they conspire against the poor husbands.

The School for Wives

"*Ninth Maxim.*

"Every woman who wishes to preserve her honour should abstain from gambling as a plague; for play is very seductive, and often drives a woman to put down her last stake.

"*Tenth Maxim.*

"She must not venture on public promenades nor picnics; for wise men are of opinion that it is always the husband who pays for such treats.

"*Eleventh Maxim—*"

Arnolphe. You shall finish it by yourself; and, by and by, I shall explain these things to you properly, word for word. I bethink myself of an engagement. I have but one word to say, and I shall not stay long. Go in again, and take special care of this volume. If the notary comes, let him wait for me a short time.

Scene III.—Arnolphe, *alone.*

I cannot do better than make her my wife. I shall be able to mould her as I please; she is like a bit of wax in my hands, and I can give her what shape I like. She was near being wiled away from me in my absence through her excess of simplicity; but, to say the truth, it is better that a wife should err on that side. The cure for these faults is easy; every simple person is docile; and if she is led out of the right way, a couple of words will instantly bring her back again. But a clever woman is quite another sort of animal. Our lot depends only on her judgment; nought can divert her from what she is set on, and our teaching in such a case is futile. Her wit avails her to ridicule our maxims, often to turn her vices into virtues, and to find means to cheat the ablest, so as to compass her own ends. We labour in vain to parry the blow; a clever woman is a devil at intrigue, and when her whim has mutely passed sentence on our honour, we must knock under. Many good fellows could tell as much. But my blundering friend shall have no cause to laugh; he has reaped the harvest of his gossip. This is the general fault of Frenchmen. When they have a love adventure, secrecy bores them, and silly vanity has so many charms for them, that they would rather hang themselves than hold their tongues. Ah! women are an easy prey to Satan when they go and choose such addle–pates! And when—But here he is—I must dissemble, and find out how he has been mortified.

Scene IV.—Horace, Arnolphe.

Horace. I am come from your house. Fate seems resolved that I shall never meet you there. But I shall go so often that some time or other—

Arnolphe. Bah, for goodness' sake, do not let us begin these idle compliments. Nothing vexes me like ceremony; and, if I could have my way, it should be abolished. It is a wretched custom, and most people foolishly waste two-thirds of their time on it. Let us put on our hats, without more ado. (*Puts on his hat.*) Well, how about your love affair? May I know, Mr. Horace, how it goes? I was diverted for a while by some business that came into my head; but since then I have been thinking of it. I admire the rapidity of your commencement, and am interested in the issue.

Horace. Indeed, since I confided in you, my love has been unfortunate.

Arnolphe. Ay! How so?

Horace. Cruel fate has brought her governor back from the country.

Arnolphe. What bad luck!

Horace. Moreover, to my great sorrow, he has discovered what has passed in private between us.

Arnolphe. How the deuce could he discover this affair so soon?

Horace. I do not know; but it certainly is so. I meant, at the usual hour, to pay a short visit to my young charmer, when, with altered voice and looks, her two servants barred my entrance, and somewhat rudely shut the door in my face, saying "Begone, you bring us into trouble!"

Arnolphe. The door in your face!

Horace. In my face.

Arnolphe. That was rather hard.

Horace. I wished to speak to them through the door; but to all I said their only answer was, "You shan't come in; master has forbidden it."

Arnolphe. Did they not open the door then?

Horace. No. And Agnès from the window made me more certain as to her master's return, by bidding me begone in a very angry tone, and flinging a stone at me into the bargain.

Arnolphe. What, a stone?

Horace. Not a small one either; that was how she rewarded my visit with her own hands.

Arnolphe. The devil! These are no trifles. Your affair seems to me in a bad way.

Horace. True, I am in a quandary through this unlucky return.

Arnolphe. Really I am sorry for you; I declare I am.

Horace. This fellow mars all.

Arnolphe. Yes, but that is nothing. You will find a way to recover yourself.

Horace. I must try by some device to baffle the strict watch of this jealous fellow.

Arnolphe. That will be easy: after all the girl loves you.

Horace. Doubtless.

Arnolphe. You will compass your end.

Horace. I hope so.

Arnolphe. The stone has put you out, but you cannot wonder at it.

Horace. True; and I understood in a moment that my rival was there, and that he was directing all without being seen. But what surprised me, and will surprise you, is another incident I am going to tell you of; a bold stroke of this lovely girl, which one could not have expected from her simplicity. Love, it must be allowed, is an able master; he teaches us to be what we never were before; a complete change in our manners is often the work of a moment under his tuition. He breaks through the impediments in our nature, and his sudden feats have the air of miracles. In an instant he makes the miser liberal, a coward brave, a churl polite. He renders the dullest soul fit for anything, and gives wit to the most simple. Yes, this last miracle is surprising in Agnès; for, blurting out these very words: "Begone, I am resolved never to receive your visits. I know all you would say, and *there* is my answer!"—this stone, or pebble, at which you are surprised, fell at my feet, with a letter. I greatly admire this note, chiming in with the significance of her words, and the casting of the stone. Are you not surprised by such an action as this? Does not love know how to sharpen the understanding? And can it be denied that his ardent flames have marvellous effects on the heart? What say you of the trick, and of the letter? Ah, do you not admire her cunning contrivance? Is it not amusing to see what a part my jealous rival has played in all this game? Say—

Arnolphe. Ay, very amusing.

Horace. Laugh at it, then. (Arnolphe *forces a laugh*.) This fellow, garrisoned against my passion, who shuts himself up in his house, and seems provided with stones, as though I were preparing to enter by storm, who, in his ridiculous terror, encourages all his household to drive me away, is tricked before his very eyes by her whom he would keep in the utmost ignorance! For my part, I confess that, although his return throws my love affair in disorder, I think all this so exceedingly comical, that I cannot forbear laughing at it whenever it comes into my head. It seems to me that you do not laugh at if half enough.

Arnolphe(*with a forced laugh*). I beg pardon; I laugh at it as much as I can.

Horace. But I must shew you her letter, for friendship's sake. Her hand knew how to set down all that her heart felt; but in such touching terms, so kind, so innocently tender, so ingenuous—in a word, just as an unaffected nature confesses its first attack of love.

Arnolphe(*softly*). This is the use you make of writing, you hussy. It was against my wish you ever learned it.

The School for Wives

Horace(*reads*). "*I wish to write to you, but I am at a loss how to begin. I have some thoughts which I should like you to know; but I do not know how to tell them to you, and I mistrust my own words. As I begin to feel that I have been always kept in ignorance, I fear to say something which is not right, and to express more than I ought. In fact I do not know what you have done to me; but I feel that I am desperately vexed at what I am made to do against you, that it will be the hardest thing in the world for me to do without you, and that I should be very glad to be with you. Perhaps it is wrong to say that, but the truth is I cannot help saying it, and I wish it could be brought about without harm. I am assured that all young men are deceivers, that they must not be listened to , and that all you told me was but to deceive me; but I assure you I have not yet come to believe that of you, and I am so touched by your words that I could not believe them false. Tell me frankly if they be: for, to be brief, as I am without an evil thought, you would be extremely wicked to deceive me, and I think I should die of vexation at such a thing .*"

Arnolphe(*aside*). Ah, the cat!

Horace. What is wrong?

Arnolphe. Wrong? Nothing! I was only coughing.

Horace. Have you ever heard a more tender expression? In spite of the cursed endeavours of unreasonable power, could you imagine a more genuine nature? Is it not beyond doubt a terrible crime villainously to mar such an admirable spirit, to try to stifle this bright soul in ignorance and stupidity? Love has begun to tear away the veil, and if, thanks to some lucky star, I can deal, as I hope, with this sheer animal, this wretch, this hang–dog, this scoundrel, this brute—

Arnolphe. Good–bye.

Horace. Why are you in such a hurry?

Arnolphe. It just occurs to me that I have a pressing engagement.

Horace. But do you not know anyone, for you live close by, who could get access to this house? I am open with you, and it is the usual thing for friends to help each other in these cases. I have no one there now except people who watch me; maid and man, as I just experienced, would not cease their rudeness and listen to me, do what I would. I had for some time in my interest an old woman of remarkable shrewdness; in fact more than human. She served me well in the beginning; but the poor woman died four days ago. Can you not devise some plan for me?

Arnolphe. No, really. You will easily find some one without me.

Horace. Good—bye then. You see what confidence I put in you.

Scene V.—Arnolphe, *alone*.

How I am obliged to suffer before him! How hard it is to conceal my gnawing pain! What! Such ready wit in a simpleton? The traitress has pretended to be so to my face, or the devil has breathed this cunning into her heart. But now that cursed letter is the death of me. I see that the rascal has corrupted her mind, and has established himself there in my stead. This is despair and deadly anguish for me. I suffer doubly by being robbed of her heart, for love as well as honour is injured by it. It drives me mad to find my place usurped, and I am enraged to see my prudence defeated. I know that to punish her guilty passion I have only to leave her to her evil fate, and that I shall be revenged on her by herself; but it is very vexatious to lose what we love. Good Heaven! after employing so much philosophy in my choice, why am I to be so terribly bewitched by her charms? She has neither relatives, friends, nor money; she abuses my care, my kindness, my tenderness; and yet I love her to distraction, even after this base trick! Fool, have you no shame? Ah, I cannot contain myself; I am mad; I could punch my head a thousand times over. I shall go in for a little; but only to see what she looks like after so vile a deed. Oh, Heaven, grant that my brow may escape dishonour; or rather, if it is decreed that I must endure it, at least grant me, under such misfortunes, that fortitude with which few are endowed.

ACT IV

Scene I.—Arnolphe, *alone*.

I declare I cannot rest anywhere; my mind is troubled by a thousand cares, thinking how to contrive, both indoors and out, so as to frustrate the attempts of this coxcomb. With what assurance the traitress stood the sight of me! She is not a whit moved by all that she has done, and though she has brought me within an inch of the grave, one could swear, to look at her, that she had no hand in it. The more composed she looked when I saw her, the more I was enraged, and those ardent transports which inflamed my heart seemed to redouble my great love for her. I was provoked, angry, incensed against her, and yet I never saw her look so lovely. Her eyes never seemed to me so bright; never before did they inspire me with such vehement desires; I feel that it will be the death of me, if my evil destiny should bring upon me this disgrace. What! I have brought her up with so much tenderness and forethought; I have had her with me from her infancy; I have indulged in the fondest hopes about her; my heart trusted to her growing charms; I have fondled her as my own for thirteen years, as I imagined—all for a young fool, with whom she is in love, to come and carry her off before my face, and that when she is already half married to me! No, by Heaven—no, by Heaven, my foolish young friend; you will be a cunning fellow to overturn my scheme, for, upon my word, all your hopes will be in vain, and you shall find no reason for laughing at me!

Scene II.—A Notary, Arnolphe.

Notary. Ah, there he is. Good–day. Here I am, ready to draw up the contract which you wish.

Arnolphe (not seeing or bearing him). How is it to be done?

Notary. It must be in the usual form.

Arnolphe (thinking himself alone). I shall take the greatest possible care.

Notary. I shall do nothing contrary to your interests.

Arnolphe (not seeing him). I must guard against all surprise.

Notary. It is enough that your affairs are placed in my hands. For fear of deception, you must not sign the contract before receiving the portion.

Arnolphe (thinking himself alone). I fear, if I let anything get abroad, that this business will become town talk.

Notary. Well, it is easy to avoid this publicity, and your contract can be drawn up privately.

Arnolphe (*thinking himself alone*). But how shall I manage it with her?

Notary. The jointure should be proportionate to the fortune she brings you.

Arnolphe (*not seeing him*). I love her, and that love is my great difficulty.

Notary. In that case the wife may have so much the more.

Arnolphe (*thinking himself alone*). How can I act towards her in such a case?

Notary. The regular way is that the husband that is to be settles on the wife that is to be a third of her marriage portion as a jointure; but this rule goes for nothing, and you may do a great deal more if you have a mind to it.

Arnolphe. If—(*seeing him*).

Notary. As for the préciput, that is a question for both sides. I say the husband can settle on his wife what he thinks proper.

Arnolphe. Eh?

Notary. He can benefit her, when he loves her much, and wishes to do her a favour, and that by way of jointure, or settlement as it is called, which is lost upon her death; either without reversion, going from her to her heirs, or by statute, as people have a mind, or by actual deed of gift in form, which may be made either single or mutual. Why do you shrug your shoulders? Am I talking like a fool, or do I not understand contracts? Who can teach me? No one, I imagine. Do I not know that when people are married, they have a joint right to all moveables, moneys, fixtures, and acquisitions, unless they resign it by act of renunciation? Do I not know that a third part of the portion of the wife that is to be becomes common, in order—

Arnolphe. Yes, verily, you know all this; but who has said one word to you about it?

Notary. You, who seem to take me for a fool, shrugging your shoulders, and making faces at me.

Arnolphe. Hang the man his beastly face! Good day: that's the way to get rid of you.

Notary. Was I not brought here to draw up a contract?

Arnolphe. Yes, I sent for you. But the business is put off; I shall send for you again when the time is fixed. What a devil of a fellow he is with his jabbering!

Notary (*alone*). I think he is mad, and I believe I am right.

Scene III.—A Notary, Alain, Georgette.

Notary. Did you not come to fetch me to your master?

Alain. Yes.

Notary. I do not know what you think; but go and tell him from me that he is a downright fool.

Georgette. We will not fail.

Scene IV.—Arnolphe, Alain, Georgette.

Georgette. Sir—

Arnolphe. Come here! You are my faithful, my good, my real friends; I have news for you.

Alain. The notary—

Arnolphe. Never mind; some other day for that. A foul plot is contrived against my honour. What a disgrace it would be for you, my children, if your master's honour were taken away! After that, you would not dare to be seen anywhere; for whoever saw you would point at you. So, since the affair concerns you as well as me, you must take care that this spark may not in any way—

Georgette. You have taught us our lesson just now.

Arnolphe. But take care not to listen to his fine speeches.

Alain. Oh, certainly—

Georgette. We know how to deny him.

Arnolphe. Suppose he should come now, wheedling: "Alain, my good fellow, cheer my drooping spirits by a little help."

Alain. You are a fool.

Arnolphe. You are right! (*To* Georgette.) "Georgette, my darling, you look so sweet—tempered and so kind!"

Georgette. You are a lout.

Arnolphe. You are right. (*To* Alain). "What harm do you find in an honest and perfectly virtuous scheme?"

Alain. You are a rogue.

Arnolphe. Capital! (*To* Georgette.) "I shall surely die if you do not take pity on my sufferings."

Georgette. You are a brazen—faced blockhead.

Arnolphe. First—rate! (*To* Alain.) "I am not one who expects something for nothing; I can remember those who serve me. Here, Alain, is a trifle in advance, to have a drink with; and, Georgette, here is wherewith to buy you a petticoat. (*Both hold out their hands and take the money.*) This is only an earnest of what I intend to do for you; I ask no other favour but that you will let me see your pretty mistress."

Georgette (*pushing him*). Try your games elsewhere.

Arnolphe. That was good.

Alain (*pushing him*). Get out of this.

Arnolphe. Very good!

Georgette (*pushing him*). Immediately!

Arnolphe. Good! Hulloa, that is enough.

Georgette. Am I not doing right?

Alain. Is this how you would have us act?

Arnolphe. Yes, capital; except for the money, which you must not take.

Georgette. We did not think of that.

Alain. Shall we begin again now?

Arnolphe. No. It is enough. Go in, both of you.

Alain. You need only say so.

Arnolphe. No, I tell you; go in when I desire you. You may keep the money. Go. I shall soon be with you again; keep your eyes open, and second my efforts.

Scene V.—Arnolphe, *alone*.

I will get the cobbler, who lives at the corner of the street, to be my spy, and tell me everything. I mean to keep her always indoors, watch her constantly—and banish in particular all sellers of ribbons, tire—women, hair—dressers, kerchief—makers, glove—sellers, dealers in cast—off apparel, and all those folks who make it their business clandestinely to bring people together who are in love. In fact, I have seen the world, and understand its tricks. My spark must be very cunning if a love–letter or message gets in here.

Scene VI.—Horace, Arnolphe.

Horace. How lucky I am to meet you here! I had a narrow escape just now, I can assure you. As I left you, I unexpectedly saw Agnès alone on her balcony, breathing the fresh air from the neighbouring trees. After giving me a sign, she contrived to come down into the garden and open the door. But we were scarcely into her room before she heard her jealous gentleman upon the stairs; and all she could do in such a case was to lock me into a large wardrobe. He entered the room at once. I did not see him, but I heard him walking up and down at a great rate, without saying a word, but sighing desperately at intervals, and occasionally thumping the table, striking a little frisky dog, and madly throwing about whatever came in his way. In his rage he broke the very vases with which the beauty had adorned her mantel–piece; doubtless the tricks she played must have come to the ears of this cuckold in embryo. At last, having in a score of ways vented his passion on things that could not help themselves, my restless jealous gentleman left the room without saying what disturbed him, and I left my wardrobe. We would not stay long together, for fear of my rival; it would have been too great a risk. But late to–night I am to enter her room without making a noise. I am to announce myself by three hems, and then the window is to be opened; whereby, with a ladder, and the help of Agnès, my love will try to gain me admittance. I tell you this as my only friend. Joy is increased by imparting it; and should we taste perfect bliss a hundred times over, It would not satisfy us unless it were known to some one. I believe you will sympathize in my success. Good–bye. I am going to make the needful preparations.

Scene VII.—Arnolphe, *alone.*

What, will the star which is bent on driving me to despair allow me no time to breathe? Am I to see, through their mutual understanding, my watchful care and my wisdom defeated one after another? Must I, in my mature age, become the dupe of a simple girl and a scatter–brained young fellow? For twenty years, like a discreet philosopher, I have been musing on the wretched fate of married men, and have carefully informed myself of the accidents which plunge the most prudent into misfortune. Profiting in my own mind by the disgrace of others, and having a wish to marry, I sought how to secure my forehead from attack, and prevent its being matched with those of other men. For this

39

noble end, I thought I had put in practice all that human policy could invent; but, as though it were decreed by fate that no man here below should be exempt from it, after all my experience and the knowledge I have been able to glean of such matters, after more than twenty years of meditation, so as to guide myself with all precaution, I have avoided the tracks of so many husbands to find myself after all involved in the same disgrace! Ah, cursed fate, you shall yet be a liar! I am still possessor of the loved one! if her heart be stolen by this obnoxious fop, I shall at least take care that he does not seize anything else. This night, which they have chosen for their pretty plan, shall not be spent so agreeably as they anticipate. It is some pleasure to me, amidst all this, to know that he has warned me of the snare he is laying, and that this blunderer, who would be my ruin, makes a confidant of his own rival.

Scene VIII.—Chrysalde, Arnolphe.

Chrysalde. Well, shall we take our supper before our walk?

Arnolphe. No, I fast to–night.

Chrysalde. Whence this fancy?

Arnolphe. Pray excuse me; there is something that hinders me.

Chrysalde. Is not your intended marriage to take place?

Arnolphe. You take too much trouble about other people's affairs.

Chrysalde. Oh ho, so snappish? What ails you? Have you encountered any little mishap in your love, my friend? By your face I could almost swear you have.

Arnolphe. Whatever happens, I shall at least have the advantage of being unlike some folks, who meekly suffer the visits of gallants.

Chrysalde. It is an odd thing that, with so much intelligence, you always get so frightened at these matters; that you set your whole happiness on this, and imagine no other kind of honour in the world. To be a miser, a brute, a rogue, wicked and cowardly, is nothing in your mind compared with this stain; and however a man may have lived, he is a man of honour if he is not a cuckold. After all, why do you imagine that our glory depends on such an accident, and that a virtuous mind must reproach itself for the evil which it cannot prevent? Tell me, why do you hold that a man in taking a wife deserves praise or blame for the choice he makes, and why do you form a frightful bugbear out of the offence caused by her want of fidelity? Be persuaded that a man of honour may have a less serious notion of cuckoldom; that as none is secure from strokes of chance, this accident ought to be a matter of indifference; and that all the evil, whatever the world may say, is in the mode of receiving it. To behave well under these difficulties, as in all else, a man must shun extremes; not ape those over–simple folks who are proud of such affairs, and are ever inviting the gallants of their wives, praising them everywhere, and crying them up, displaying their sympathy with them, coming to all their entertainments and all their meetings, and making everyone wonder at their having the assurance to show their faces there. This way of acting is no doubt highly culpable; but the other extreme is no less to be condemned. If I do not approve of such as are the friends of their wives' gallants; no more do I approve of your violent men whose indiscreet resentment, full of rage and fury, draws the eyes of all the world on them by its noise, and who seem, from their outbreaks, unwilling that any one should be ignorant of what is wrong with them. There is a mean between these extremes, where a wise man stops in such a case. When we know how to take it, there is no reason to blush for the worst a woman can do to us. In short, say what you will, cuckolding may easily be made to seem less terrible; and, as I told you before, all your dexterity lies in being able to turn the best side outwards.

Arnolphe. After this fine harangue, all the brotherhood owes your worship thanks; any one who hears you speak will be delighted to enrol himself.

Chrysalde. I do not say that; for that is what I have found fault with. But as fortune gives us a wife, I say that we should act as we do when we gamble with dice, when, if you do not get what you want, you must be shrewd and good–tempered, to amend your luck by good management.

Arnolphe. That is, sleep and eat well, and persuade yourself that it is all nothing.

Chrysalde. You think to make a joke of it; but, to be candid, I know a hundred things in the world more to be dreaded, and which I should think a much greater misfortune, than the accident you are so grievously afraid of. Do you think that, in choosing between the

41

two alternatives, I should not prefer to be what you say, rather than see myself married to one of those good creatures whose ill–humour makes a quarrel out of nothing—those dragons of virtue, those respectable she–devils, ever piquing themselves on their wise conduct, who, because they do not do us a trifling wrong, take on themselves to behave haughtily, and, because they are faithful to us, expect that we should bear everything for them? Once more, my friend, know that cuckoldom is just what we make of it, that on some accounts it is even to be desired, and that it has its pleasures like other things.

Arnolphe. If you are of a mind to be satisfied with it, I am not disposed to try it myself; and rather than submit to such a thing—

Chrysalde. Bless me! do not swear, lest you should be forsworn. If fate has willed it, your precautions are useless; and your advice will not be taken in the matter.

Arnolphe. I!—I a cuckold!

Chrysalde. You are in a bad way. A thousand folks are so—I mean no offence—who, for bearing, courage, fortune and family, would scorn comparison with you.

Arnolphe. And I, on my side, will not draw comparisons with them. But, let me tell you, this pleasantry annoys me. Let us have done with it, if you please.

Chrysalde. You are in a passion. We shall know the cause. Good–bye; but remember, whatever your honour prompts you to do in this business, to swear you will never be what we have talked of is half–way towards being it.

Arnolphe. And I swear it again! I am going this instant to find a good remedy against such an accident.

Scene IX.—Arnolphe, Alain, Georgette.

Arnolphe. My friends, now is the time that I beg your assistance. I am touched by your affection; but it must be well proved on this occasion; and if you serve me in this, as I am sure you will, you may count on your reward. The man you wot of (but not a word!) seeks, as I understand, to trick me this very night, and enter, by a ladder, into Agnès' room. But we three must lay a trap for him. I would have each of you take a good cudgel, and, when he shall be nearly on the top round of the ladder (for I shall open the window at the proper time), both of you shall fall on the rascal for me, so that his back may be sure to remember it, in order that he may learn never to come here again. Yet do it without naming me in any way, or making it appear that I am behind. Would you have the courage to execute my resentment?

Alain. If the thrashing is all, sir, rely on us. You shall see, when I beat, if I am a slow coach.

Georgette. Though my arm may not look so strong, it shall play its part in the drubbing.

Arnolphe. Get you in, then; and, above all, mind you do not chatter. (*Alone.*) This is a useful lesson for my neighbours; if all the husbands in town were to receive their wives' gallants in this fashion, the number of cuckolds would not be so great.

ACT V

Scene I.—Arnolphe, Alain, Georgette.

Arnolphe. Wretches! what have you done by your violence?

Alain. We have obeyed you, sir.

Arnolphe. It is of no use trying to defend yourselves by such an excuse. My orders were to beat him, not to murder him. I told you to discharge your blows on his back, and not on his head. Good Heavens! into what a plight my fate has now thrown me! And what course can I take, as the man is dead? Go into the house, and be sure to say nothing of the harmless order that I gave you. (*Alone.*) It will be daylight presently, and I shall go and consider how to bear myself under this misfortune. Alas! what will become of me? And what will Horace's father say when he shall suddenly hear of this affair?

Scene II.—Arnolphe, Horace.

Horace (*aside*). I must go and make out who it is.

The School for Wives

Arnolphe (*thinking himself alone*). Could one ever have foreseen— (*Running against* Horace.) Who is there, pray?

Horace. Is it you, M. Arnolphe?

Arnolphe. Yes; but who are you?

Horace. Horace. I was going to your house to beg a favour. You are out very early.

Arnolphe (*to himself aside*). Wonderful! Is it magic? Is it a vision?

Horace. To tell the truth, I was in a great difficulty; I thank Heaven's great goodness that at the nick of time I thus meet you. Let me tell you that everything has succeeded, much better even than I could have predicted, and by an accident which might have spoiled all. I do not know how our appointment could possibly have been suspected; but just as I was reaching the window, I unluckily saw some persons, who, unceremoniously raising their hand against me, made me miss my footing, and fall to the ground, which, at the expense of a bruise, saved me from a score of blows. These people, of whom, I fancy, my jealous rival was one, attributed my fall to their blows, and as the pain compelled me to lie for some time motionless, they honestly thought they had killed me, and were greatly alarmed. I heard all their noise in profound silence. Each, accusing the other of the violence, and complaining of their ill fortune, came softly, without a light, to feel if I were dead. You may imagine that I contrived in the darkness of night, to assume the appearance of a real corpse. They went away in great terror; and as I was thinking how I should make my escape, the young Agnès, frightened by my pretended death, came to me in great concern. For the talking of those people had reached her ears from the very first, and, being unobserved during all this commotion, she easily escaped from the house. But finding me unhurt, she displayed a transport which it would be difficult to describe. What more need I say? The lovely girl obeyed the promptings of her affection, would not return to her room, and commited her fate to my honour. You may judge, from this instance of innocence, to what she is exposed by the mad intolerance of a fool, and what frightful risks she might have run, if I were a man to hold her less dear than I do. But too pure a passion fills my soul; I would rather die than wrong her. I see in her charms worthy of a better fate, and nought but death shall part us. I foresee the rage my father will be in. But we must find an opportunity to appease his anger. I cannot help being transported by charms so delightful; and, in short, we must in this life be satisfied with our lot. What I wish you to do, as a confidential friend, is to let me place this beauty under your care; and that, in the interest of my love, you will conceal her in your house for at least a day or two. For, besides that I must conceal her flight from every one, to prevent any successful pursuit of her, you know that a young girl, especially such a beautiful one, would be strongly suspected in the company of a young man; and as I have trusted the whole secret of my passion to you, being assured of your prudence, so to you only, as a generous friend, can I confide this beloved treasure.

Arnolphe. Be assured I am entirely at your service.

Horace. You will really do me so great a favour?

Arnolphe. Very willingly, I tell you; I am delighted at the opportunity of serving you. I thank Heaven for putting it in my way; I never did anything with so much pleasure.

Horace. How much I am obliged to you for all your kindness! I feared a difficulty on your part; but you know the world, and your wisdom can excuse the ardour of youth. One of my servants is with her at the corner of this street.

Arnolphe. But how shall we manage, for day begins to break? If I take her here, I may be seen; and if you come to my house the servants will talk. To take a safe course you must bring her to me in a darker place. That alley of mine is convenient; I shall wait for her there.

Horace. It is quite right to use these precautions. I shall only place her in your hands, and return at once to my lodgings, without more ado.

Arnolphe(*alone*). Ah, fortune! This propitious accident makes amends for all the mischief which your caprice has done! (He *muffles himself up in his cloak*.)

Scene III.—Agnès, Horace, Arnolphe.

Arnolphe. (to Agnès). Do not be uneasy at the place I am taking you to. I conduct you to a safe abode. It would ruin all for you to lodge with me. Go in at this door, and follow where you are led. (ARNOLPHE *takes her hand, without being recognised by her*.)

Agnès (*to* Horace). Why do you leave me?

Horace. Dear Agnès, it must be so.

Agnès. Remember, then, I pray you to return soon.

Horace. My love urges me sufficiently for that.

Agnès. I feel no joy but when I see you.

Horace. Away from you I also am sad.

Agnès. Alas, if that were so, you would stay here.

Horace. What! Can you doubt my excessive love?

Agnès. No; you do not love me as much as I love you! Ah, he is pulling me too hard! (Arnolphe *pulls her away*).

Horace. It is because it is dangerous, dear Agnès, for us to be seen together here; this true friend, whose hand draws you away, acts with the prudent zeal that inspires him on our behalf.

Agnès. But to follow a stranger—

Horace. Fear nothing. In such hands you cannot but be safe.

Agnès. I would rather be in Horace's; and I should—(*To* Arnolphe, *who still drags her away*). Stay a little.

Horace. Farewell. The day drives me away.

Agnès. When shall I see you, then?

Horace. Very soon, you may be sure.

Agnès. How weary I shall be till I do!

HORACE (*going*). Thank Heaven, my happiness is no longer in suspense; now I can sleep securely.

Scene IV.—Arnolphe, Agnès.

Arnolphe (*concealed by his cloak, and disguising his voice*). Come; it is not there you are going to lodge. I have provided a room for you elsewhere, and intend to place you where you will be safe enough. (*Discovering himself.*) Do you know me?

Agnès. Ah!

Arnolphe. My face frightens you now, hussy; it is a disappointment to you to see me here. I interrupt your love and its pretty contrivances. (Agnès *looks for* Horace). Do not imagine you can call your lover to your aid with those eyes of yours; he is too far off to give you any assistance. So, so! young as you are, You can play such pranks. Your simplicity, that seemed so extraordinary, asks if infants come through the ear; yet you manage to make an assignation by night, and to slink out silently in order to follow your gallant? Gad, how coaxing your tongue was with him! You must have been at a good school. Who the deuce has taught you so much all on a sudden? You are no longer afraid, then, to meet ghosts; this gallant has given you courage in the night time. Ah, baggage, to arrive at such a pitch of deceit! To form such a plot in spite of all my kindness! Little serpent that I have warmed in my bosom, and that as soon as it feels it is alive, tries ungratefully to injure him that cherished it!

Agnès. Why do you scold me?

Arnolphe. Of a truth, I do wrong!

Agnès. I am not conscious of harm in all that I have done.

Arnolphe. To run after a gallant is not, then, an infamous thing?

Agnès. He is one who says he wishes to marry me. I followed your directions; you can have taught me that we ought to marry in order to avoid sin.

47

Arnolphe. Yes; but I meant to take you to wife myself; I think I gave you to understand it clearly enough.

Agnès. You did. But, to be frank with you, he is more to my taste for a husband than you. With you, marriage is a trouble and a pain, and your descriptions give a terrible picture of it; but there—he makes it seem so full of joy that I long to marry.

Arnolphe. Oh, traitress, that is because you love him!

Agnès. Yes, I love him.

Arnolphe. And you have the impudence to tell me so!

Agnès. Why, if it is true, should I not say so?

Arnolphe. Ought you to love him, minx?

Agnès. Alas! can I help it? He alone is the cause of it; I was not thinking of it when it came about.

Arnolphe. But you ought to have driven away that amorous desire.

Agnès. How can we drive away what gives us pleasure?

Arnolphe. And did you not know that it would displease me?

Agnès. I? Not at all. What harm can it do you?

Arnolphe. True. I ought to rejoice at it. You do not love me then after all?

Agnès. You?

Arnolphe. Yes.

Agnès. Alack! no.

The School for Wives

Arnolphe. How! No?

Agnès. Would you have me tell a fib?

Arnolphe. Why not love me, Madam Impudence?

Agnès. Heaven! you ought not to blame me. Why did you not make yourself loved, as he has done? I did not prevent you, I fancy.

Arnolphe. I tried all I could; but all my pains were to no purpose.

Agnès. Of a truth then he knows more about it than you; for he had no difficulty in making himself loved.

Arnolphe (aside). See how the jade reasons and retorts! Plague! could one of your witty ladies say more about it? Ah, I was a dolt; or else, on my honour, a fool of a girl knows more than the wisest, man. (*To* Agnès.) Since you are so good at reasoning, Madam Chop–logic, should I have maintained you so long for his benefit?

Agnès. No. He will pay you back, even to the last farthing.

Arnolphe (aside). She hits on words that double my vexation. (*Aloud*). With all his ability, hussy, will he discharge me the obligations that you owe me?

Agnès. I do not owe you so much as you may think.

Arnolphe. Was the care of bringing you up nothing?

Agnès. Verily, you have been at great pains there, and have caused me to be finely taught throughout. Do you think I flatter myself so far as not to know in my own mind that I am an ignoramus? I am ashamed of myself, and at my age, I do not wish to pass any longer for a fool, if I can help it.

Arnolphe. You shrink from ignorance, and would learn something of your spark, at any cost.

Agnès. To be sure. It is from him I know what I do know; I fancy I owe him much more than you.

Arnolphe. Really, what prevents me from revenging this saucy talk with a cuff? I am enraged at the sight of her provoking coldness: and to beat her would be a satisfaction to me.

Agnès. Ah, you can do that if you choose.

Arnolphe (*aside*). That speech and that look disarm my fury, and bring back the tenderness to my heart which effaces all her guilt. How strange it is to be in love! To think that men should be subject to such weakness for these traitresses! Everyone knows their imperfection. They are extravagant and indiscreet. Their mind is wicked and their understanding weak. There is nought weaker, more imbecile, more faithless; and, in spite of all, everything in the world is done for the sake of these bipeds. (*To* Agnès). Well, let us make peace. Listen, little wretch, I forgive all, and restore you to my affection. Learn thus how much I love you; and, seeing me so good, love me in return.

Agnès. With all my heart I should like to please you, if it were in my power.

Arnolphe. Poor little darling, you can if you will. Just listen to this sigh of love. See this dying look, behold my person, and forsake this young coxcomb and the love he inspires. He must have thrown some spell over you, and you will be a hundred times happier with me. Your desire is to be finely dressed and frolicsome; then I swear you shall ever be so; I will fondle you night and day, I will hug you, kiss you, devour you; you shall do everything you have a mind to. I do not enter into particulars; and that is saying everything. (*Aside*). To what length will my passion go? (*Aloud*). In short, nothing can equal my love. What proof would you have me give you, ungrateful girl? Would you have me weep? Shall I beat myself? Shall I tear out one half of my hair? Shall I kill myself? Yes, say so if you will. I am quite ready, cruel creature, to convince you of my love.

Agnès. Stay. All you say does not touch my heart. Horace could do more with a couple of words.

The School for Wives

Arnolphe. Ah, this is too great an insult, and provokes my anger too far. I will pursue my design, you intractable brute, and will pack you out of the town forthwith. You reject my addresses and drive me to extremities: but the innermost cell of a convent shall avenge me of all.

Scene V.—Arnolphe, Agnès, Alain.

Alain. I do not know how it is, master, but it seems to me that Agnès and the corpse have run away together.

Arnolphe. She is here. Go and shut her up in my room. (*Aside*). Horace will not come here to see her. Besides, it is only for half an hour. (*To* ALAIN). Go and get a carriage, for I mean to find her a safe dwelling. Shut yourself safely in, and, above all, do not take your eyes off her. (*Alone*). Perhaps when her mind is buried in solitude, she will be disabused of this passion.

Scene VI.—Horace, Arnolphe.

Horace. Oh, I come here, plunged in grief. Heaven, Mr.Arnolphe has decreed my ill fortune! By a fatal stroke of extreme justice, I am to be torn away from the beauty whom I love. My father arrived this very evening. I found him alighting close by. In a word the reason of his coming, with which, as I said, I was unacquainted, is, that he has made a match for me, without a word of warning; he has arrived here to celebrate the nuptials. Feel for my anxiety, and judge if a more cruel disappointment could happen to me. That Enrique, whom I asked you about Yesterday, is the source of all my trouble. He has come with my father to complete my ruin; it is for his only daughter that I am destined. I thought I should have swooned when they first spoke of it; not caring to hear more, as my father spoke of paying you a visit, I hurried here before him, my mind full of consternation. I pray you be sure not to let him know anything of my engagement, which might incense him; and try, since he has confidence in you, to dissuade him from this other match.

Arnolphe. Ay, to be sure!

Horace. Advise him to delay; and thus, like a friend, help me in my passion.

Arnolphe. No fear!

Horace. All my hope is in you.

Arnolphe. It could not be better placed.

Horace. I look on you as my real father. Tell him that my age — Ah, I see him coming. Hear the arguments I can supply you with.

Scene VII.—Enrique, Oronte, Chrysalde, Horace, Arnolphe.

(Horace *and* Arnolphe *retire to the back of the stage and whisper together.*)

Enrique (*to* Chrysalde). As soon as I saw you, before anyone could tell me, I should have known you. I recognise in your face the features of your lovely sister, whom marriage made mine in former days. Happy should I have been if cruel fate had permitted me to bring back that faithful wife, to enjoy with me the great delight of seeing once more, after our continual misfortunes, all her former friends. But since the irresistible power of destiny has for ever deprived us of her dear presence, let us try to submit, and to be content with the only fruit of love which remains to me. It concerns you nearly; without your consent I should do wrong in wishing to dispose of this pledge. The choice of the son of Oronte is honourable in itself; but you must be pleased with this choice as well as I.

Chrysalde. It would argue a poor opinion of my judgment to doubt my approbation of so reasonable a choice.

Arnolphe(*aside to* Horace). Ay, I will serve you finely!

Horace. Beware, once more—

Arnolphe. Have no uneasiness. *Leaves* Horace, *and goes up to embrace* Oronte.)

Oronte. Ah, this is indeed a tender embrace.

Arnolphe. How delighted I am to see you!

Oronte. I am come here—

Arnolphe. I know what brings you, without your telling me.

Oronte. You have already heard?

Arnolphe. Yes.

Oronte. So much the better.

Arnolphe. Your son is opposed to this match; his heart being pre–engaged, he looks on it as a misfortune. He has even prayed me to dissuade you from it; for my part, all the advice I can give you is, to exert a father's authority, and not allow the marriage to be delayed. Young people should be managed with a high hand; we do them harm by being indulgent.

Horace(*aside*). Oh, the traitor!

Chrysalde. If it is repugnant to him, I think we ought not to force him. I think my brother will be of my mind.

Arnolphe. What? Will he let himself be ruled by his son? Would you have a father so weak as to be unable to make his son obey him? It would be fine indeed to see him at his time of life receiving orders from one who ought to receive them from him. No, no, he is my intimate friend, and his honour is my own. His word is passed, and he must keep it. Let him now display his firmness, and control his son's affections.

Oronte. You speak well; in this match I will answer for my son's obedience.

Chrysalde (*to* Arnolphe). I am indeed surprised at the great eagerness which you shew for this marriage, and cannot guess what is your motive—

Arnolphe. I know what I am about, and speak sensibly.

Oronte. Yes, yes, M. Arnolphe; he is—

Chrysalde. That name annoys him. He is Monsieur de la Souche, as you were told before.

Oronte. It makes no difference.

Horace (*aside*). What do I hear?

Arnolphe (*turning to* Horace). Ay, that is the mystery; you can judge as to what it behooved me to do.

Horace (*aside*). What a scrape—

Scene VIII.—Enrique, Oronte, Chrysalde, Horace, Arnolphe, Georgette.

Georgette. Sir, if you do not come, we shall scarcely be able to hold Agnès; she is trying all she can to get away; I fear she will throw herself out of the window.

Arnolphe. Bring her to me, for I mean to take her away. (*To* HORACE). Do not be disturbed. Continual good fortune makes a man proud. Every dog has his day, as the proverb says.

Horace (*aside*). Good Heaven, what misfortune can equal mine? Was ever a man in such a mess as this?

Arnolphe (*to* Oronte). Hasten the day of the ceremony. I am bent on it, and invite myself beforehand.

Oronte. That is just my intention.

Scene IX.—Agnès, Oronte, Enrique, Arnolphe, Horace, Chrysalde, Alain, Georgette.

Arnolphe (*to* Agnès). Come hither, my beauty, whom they cannot hold, and who rebels. Here is your gallant, to whom, to make amends, you may make a sweet and humble curtsey. (*To* Horace). Farewell. The issue rather thwarts your desires; but all lovers are not fortunate.

Agnès. Horace, will you let me be carried off in this manner?

The School for Wives

Horace. I scarcely know where I am, my sorrow is so great.

Arnolphe. Come along, chatterbox.

Agnès. I shall stay here.

Oronte. Tell us the meaning of this mystery. We are all staring at each other without being able to understand.

Arnolphe. I shall inform you at a more convenient time. Till then, good—bye.

Oronte. Where are you going? You do not speak to us as you should.

Arnolphe. I have advised you to complete the marriage, let Horace grumble as much as he likes.

Oronte. Ay; but to complete it, have you not heard—if they have told you all—that the lady concerned in this affair is in your house?—that she is the daughter of Enrique and of the lovely Angelica, who were privately married? Now, what was at the bottom of your talk just now?

Chrysalde. I too was astonished at his proceedings.

Arnolphe. What?

Chrysalde. My sister had a daughter by a secret marriage, whose existence was concealed from the whole family.

Oronte. And in order that nothing might be discovered, she was put out to nurse in the country by her husband, under a feigned name.

Chrysalde. At that time, fortune being against him, he was compelled to quit his native land.

Oronte. To encounter a thousand various dangers in far—distant countries, and beyond many seas.

55

Chrysalde. Where his industry has acquired what in his own land he lost through roguery and envy.

Oronte. And when he returned to France, the first thing he did was to seek out her to whom he had confided the care of his daughter.

Chrysalde. This country–woman frankly told him that she had committed her to your keeping from the age of four.

Oronte. And that she did it because she received money from you, and was very poor.

Chrysalde. Oronte, transported with joy, has even brought this woman hither.

Oronte. In short, you shall see her here directly to clear up this mystery to every one.

Chrysalde (to Arnolphe). I can almost imagine what is the cause of your grief; but fortune is kind to you. If it seems so good to you not to be a cuckold, your only course is not to marry.

Arnolphe (going away full of rage, and unable to speak). Ugh! ugh! ugh!

Scene X.—Enrique, Oronte, Chrysalde, Agnès, Horace.

Oronte. Why does he run away without saying a word?

Horace. Ah, father, you shall know the whole of this surprising mystery. Accident has done here what your wisdom intended. I had engaged myself to this beauty in the sweet bonds of mutual love; it is she, in a word, whom you come to seek, and for whose sake I was about to grieve you by my refusal.

Enrique. I was sure of it as soon as I saw her; my heart has yearned for her ever since. Ah, daughter, I am overcome by such tender transports!

Chrysalde. I could be so, brother, just as well as you. But this is hardly the place for it. Let us go inside, and clear up these mysteries. Let us shew our friend some return for his great pains, and thank Heaven, which orders all for the best.

CPSIA information can be obtained at www.ICGtesting.com
Printed in the USA
LVOW051623100112

263232LV00011B/36/P

9 781169 212800